T0198403

GRANDPA ERNEST'S PLACE:

WHERE DREAMS COME TRUE

ERNEST WASHINGTON

Archway Publishing books may be ordered through booksellers or by contacting:

Archway Publishing
1663 Liberty Drive
Bloomington, IN 47403
www.archwaypublishing.com
844-669-3957

Because of the dynamic nature of the Internet, any web addresses or links contained in this book may have changed since publication and may no longer be valid. The views expressed in this work are solely those of the author and do not necessarily reflect the views of the publisher, and the publisher hereby disclaims any responsibility for them.

Any people depicted in stock imagery provided by Getty Images are models, and such images are being used for illustrative purposes only. Certain stock imagery © Getty Images.

ISBN: 978-1-6657-4711-0 (sc)
978-1-6657-4710-3 (e)

Library of Congress Control Number: 2023913335

Print information available on the last page.

Archway Publishing rev. date: 09/29/2023

Dedication

This book is dedicated to my mom, Ernestine Washington, who instilled hope in me, telling me that I could do anything I wanted to do. She told me that God made something for everyone to do and that I must believe in myself and never stop dreaming.

About the Author

Ernest Washington was born in Jersey City, New Jersey, and grew up in Newark, New Jersey, in Stella Wrights Project. His education began at Charlton Street School, and he graduated from Central High School, in Newark, New Jersey, in 1981. He now works in human resources.

Contents

Chapter One

GRANDPA ERNEST PLAYS WHERE DREAMS COME TRUE.

Hello, kids!

My name is Ernest Washington. I know of a place where dreams come true. There, you can become whatever you want.

Amazing, isn't it?

Do you want to know where that place is and how I found it?

Keep reading.

* * *

It was a warm and quiet summer night. My wife and I were asleep. But during the middle of the night, I woke up due to throbbing pain in my right leg. I tried to touch my leg, but there was nothing. I remembered that doctors had removed my right leg a few days ago because I had developed an incurable wound. So the pain was actually in my residual limb.[1]

I was very upset. I looked up at the ceiling and started talking to God.

"Why am I like this, God? Why did they have to take my leg off? Why can't I live like other people?"

---

[1] A residual limb is the remaining part of the leg after the leg is removed.

I kept talking to God for a while, and then I got out of my bed. With the help of my walking sticks, I walked outside. It was dark. But I noticed that the caged basketball court in my backyard at the back of my house was lit up.

Who is here at this time? I thought, and I headed to the basketball court. As I entered the court, I felt sudden energy within my body. I felt strong and healthy. When I looked down, to my surprise, my right leg was back. Both of my legs were strong, and I could walk without my walking sticks.

"Wow!" I exclaimed.

A few guys were playing basketball on the court. When they saw me, they came to me, and one of them said, "Do you want to play with us?"

"Yes," I answered and started playing.

I was running, jumping, and shooting the ball like I was a teenager. When I finished playing basketball, I asked God, "God, can I stay here forever so that I can live a normal life with both my legs?"

"No, Ernest. You must go back home. You have a wife and other family members who love you a lot. What would they do without you? You are very important to them, more than you know."

I realized God was right. My wife and my dear family members loved me a lot. They were always worried for me.

"You are right, God. I understand. My family needs me," I said. Then I went back home and got in my bed again. I was so happy to have found this place where I could live my dream. It was fun. I was not upset anymore. I closed my eyes and fell asleep.

Chapter Two

Hi, kids!

I am Ernest Washington, and I am back with another story.

I drive a bus that picks up disabled kids from their homes, takes them to their appointments, and drops them off back home. All these kids call me Grandpa Ernest because I love them so much, and they love me too. If you want, you can also call me Grandpa Ernest.

One hot summer day, I picked up all the kids from their homes. We were going to enjoy some ice cream that day. All the kids were happy, but I noticed that one of the kids named Sam looked very sad.

"Why are you so upset, Sam?" I asked.

"Grandpa Ernest, why am I like this? Life is not fair. I don't want to be like this," Sam said while crying.

I dropped all the kids back home except Sam. Now, only Sam and I were left on the bus.

I looked at Sam and said, "Sam, suppose I can take you to a place where dreams come, and you can do just anything you want; what would you like to be?"

"A track star in the Olympics. I would win the one-hundred-meter race, stand on the stage, and win gold for my country." Sam looked excited.

I took Sam to the caged basketball court behind my house. As Sam walked into the cage, his physical disability was gone. He was dancing with joy.

"What place is this, Grandpa Ernest?"

"A place where dreams come true." I smiled.

Sam looked at himself and was surprised to see that he had a red shirt and blue shorts on. His shirt had letters USA printed on it in white. The track coach came over to Sam and said, "Come on, Sam; you're up next. Come and win this gold for your country."

Sam gave me a big hug and said, "Grandpa, I love you." Tears ran down his face.

Sam lined up, and as the whistle blew, he started to run toward the finishing line with all his power. Sam broke the world record and won the gold. He walked around the arena with the red, white, and blue American around him.

"America, this is for you," he screamed with enthusiasm. Then he got on the stage with tears in his eyes.

While receiving his gold medal, Sam found me in a crowd of thousands. He pointed to me and said, "Grandpa Ernest, I love you."

Everyone was happy and praising Sam.

After everything was over, Sam and I sat down on a bench.

"I don't want to leave this place, Grandpa," Sam said.

"You can stay here, my boy. There are lots of people who love you and need you in their lives. What would your mom, dad, and siblings do without you?"

"You are right." Sam understood my point. So we left the cage and headed to the bus so I could drop Sam off at home. Before getting on the bus, Sam turned around and looked at the cage. He pumped his fist and screamed, "Yes!"

Sam was delighted because he had finally lived his dream.

Chapter Three

H i, kids!

Grandpa Earnest is back with another story.

It was a moderately cold day. As usual, I was on my way to pick up the kids. First of all, I picked Lu. She was a kid who always had a smile on her face. She brought energy and joy to everyone she met. Lu always cracked jokes to make others happy. She liked to sit in the middle of the bus so that everyone could see and hear her.

But something was different that day; she seemed sad and was very quiet. She got on the bus and directly went to the back without greeting or smiling at anyone.

Lu did not even greet me; that worried me a little. I picked up the rest of the kids and took them to their appointments. Later, when I picked them up, I took all the kids to get cotton candy before dropping them off at home. I noticed that Lu did not get off the bus to get her cotton candy. So I bought one for her, and when I got back on the bus, I placed the cotton candy next to her.

While dropping the other kids at their homes, I kept observing Lu from the rearview mirror. She kept a sad face all the way along. I did not feel good while seeing her that way, so I came up with a fantastic idea.

I decided to take her to the magical place where dreams came true. After dropping off all the other kids, I went to the back of the bus and asked Lu, "Why are you so sad today?"

"Grandpa Ernest, I am tired of being like this; why can't I be normal like the other kids my age?" she answered me with hopeless eyes.

"Lu, if you can be anything in this world, what would you want to be?" I asked her.

"I would love to be a nurse. I would love to help people get better. I hope to put smiles on their faces." She looked at me and smiled.

I asked her, "Suppose I can take you to a place where dreams come true, and you can be a nurse. Would you like to go to this place?"

Excited, she said, "Yes."

So I drove her to my place. First, we went to the backyard, and then we entered the cage where dreams came true. As Lu entered the cage, it turned into a hospital. She suddenly became a nurse wearing a white uniform, and she was able to walk.

She was delighted. She gave me a big hug and said, "I love you, Grandpa Earnest."

Then we heard her name being called over the loudspeaker, "Lu, now you are needed in room 117."

She enthusiastically said, "That's me; I got to go. I will see you later, Grandpa."

In a while, I could see Nurse Lu roaming around from one room to another, helping and taking care of patients and putting smiles on their faces. Everyone loved her cheerful nature and happy spirit. I was also glad to see her live the dream of her life.

After her shift was over, she came and sat next to me. "I am staying here forever, and I don't want to go back."

"You can't stay here, my dear Lu. Many people need you. Think about your dad, mom, and brother; what would they do without you? They love you so much, and I thought you loved them too. You don't leave people you love." I made her understand calmly.

She smiled and said, "You are right, Grandpa Ernest; let's go home!"

So we left. Lu was smiling while returning to the bus. She was happy to go back home and be with her family because they loved her so much and she loved them too. As she got on the bus, she went back to pick up her cotton candy. Then, she came up to the front of the bus with me and started eating. I could see the satisfaction in her actions, and it made me relieved.

Before she got off the bus, she gave me a big hug and said, "I love you, Grandpa; thank you for an amazing experience. I will never forget it."

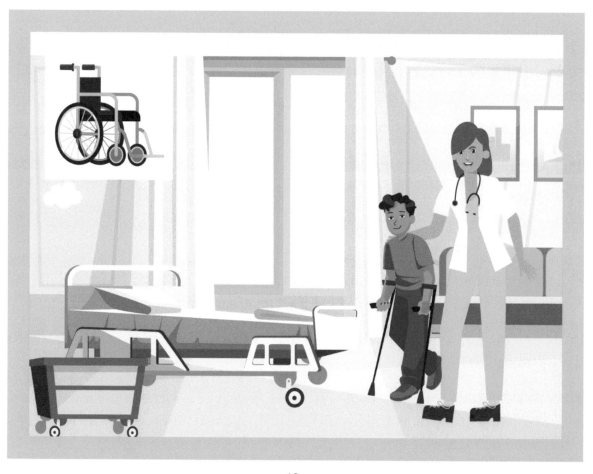

Chapter Four

Hi, kids!

Grandpa Earnest is back again with a different exciting story.

It was one of the coldest days of January. I had already had picked up a couple of kids, and now it was time to pick up Megan. When she came, I was surprised to see her puffy eyes. It seemed she had been crying.

When she got on the bus, she did not greet me. Instead, she directly went to her seat and settled down. I took all the kids to their appointments. Later, I decided to take all the kids to the arcade to play some games there. Also, I bought pizza for all of them. I knew Megan loved pizza and that she would be happy to have some.

To my surprise, she hardly had two bites and left the rest uneaten. That was when I knew something was not right with her. I murmured to myself, "I think I know how to fix this. I will take her to the cage where dreams come true."

After I had dropped off all the other kids, I went to the back of the bus and sat next to Megan. I asked her, "What is wrong, my dear Megan? It looks like you have been crying lately."

"I am tired of being like this, and it is hard to get over anything. I am legally blind, and I really can't see anything. It seems like everything is blurry. I don't know what anything looks like," Megan said. She was sobbing.

I asked her, "If you could be anything in this lifetime, what would you want to be?"

She said, "Grandpa, I would love to be a photographer. I would take pictures of everything pretty that resides in this world."

"Suppose I can you take you to a place where dreams come true, and you could be a photographer. Would you like to go to this place?"

Megan nearly jumped out of her skin and said, "Yes, Grandpa, please take me to that place right now."

So I drove her to my place. We first went to the backyard and then entered the cage where dreams came true. As she entered the cage, she just said, "Wow."

We were in Africa, and she was mesmerized to see all the pretty animals and trees. She took the camera from around her neck and took pictures of all the animals and trees she could see. She said, "These are the most beautiful sights a person could ever see."

I said, "Close your eyes and open them back up again."

When she opened her eyes, we were in Venezuela. Megan was very happy at that moment. She got busy taking more pictures. Every time she closed and reopened her eyes, we were at different places in the world.

We sat on top of Mount Everest. Megan said, "My eyes haven't seen much, but these are prettiest things they have ever seen."

I was quite happy to see her.

"Okay, Megan. It is time to go home," I said.

"No, Grandpa, I am never leaving this place." She insisted on staying.

"My dear Megan, what about your family? Don't you love them? You don't leave people you love," I said.

"You are right, Grandpa. What would they do without me? They would be worried and stay unhappy. I am the only peacemaker in my house," she replied.

So we left the cage.

"I still have the camera, Grandpa. I could show all these great pictures to my family. My older sister will go crazy for all of this," Megan said.

When we got back on the bus, she picked up her leftover pizza and started eating it.

"That's my girl; eat it all up. Love you, Megan!" I exclaimed.

She smiled and happily finished the last bite of her pizza. Before she got off the bus, she gave me a big hug and said, "I love you, Grandpa. This was indeed the best day of my life."

If any kids want their stories to be told, email me at:

grandpaernestdreamscometrue@gmail.com

with your story and a picture of yourself, along with your dream.

Love,

Grandpa Ernest

Printed in the United States
by Baker & Taylor Publisher Services